INFINITE IN FINITE

Andrew Wynn Owen's first collection, *The Multiverse*, was published in 2018. He received the Newdigate Prize in 2014 and an Eric Gregory Award in 2015.

Infinite in Finite

ANDREW WYNN OWEN

CARCANET POETRY

First published in Great Britain in 2023 by
Carcanet
Alliance House, 30 Cross Street
Manchester, M2 7AQ
www.carcanet.co.uk

A CIP catalogue record for this book is
available from the British Library.

ISBN 978 1 80017 347 7

Book design by LiteBook Prepress Services
Printed in Great Britain by SRP Ltd, Exeter, Devon

The publisher acknowledges financial
assistance from Arts Council England.

'I *know* that I don't make out my conception by my language—all poetry being a putting the infinite within the finite.'

— Robert Browning, 'RB to John Ruskin' (Paris, Dec. 10th 1855)

'Finite—to fail, but infinite—to Venture—'

— Emily Dickinson, Fr. 952

'The idea in my mind is a finite object: can it not be interpreted as determining a quus function, rather than a plus function?'

— Saul Kripke, *Wittgenstein on Rules and Private Language* (1982)

CONTENTS

INFINITE IN FINITE

APPEARANCE AND REALITY (1)

1. Consolidation

I um and om until my lifespan passes.
      I watch athletic light
   Diffract cylindrically through glasses
     Left resting on the bright
Countertop here, where I greet the new day.
    It is unfolding, is a sight,
And I am surely happy, in my way,
       To have observed
       The blazing tourniquet
       That has long served
To bind our world from losing blood,
      As on the curved
Surface of glass, and on the stagnant flood.

2. Keeping track

Optical process, not hallucination,
     Is how I gauge events.
   From there I ascertain relation,
     Within the bounds of sense,
Between the objects that appear to me,
    Keeping track of the present tense
And cautious not to slip unconsciously
       Out of its stream.
      If I did that, you see,
       The view might seem
Reliable, but I would live
      A kind of dream
And something or someone would have to give.

3. HARMONY

Many's the time I looked across the world
    And saw no answer there.
     But there is harder reason, furled
      In being's inner lair:
A boast too mythological to see,
    With footprints leading everywhere,
Born of the pre-established harmony
      Between our dreams
     And life's reliquary—
      Or so it seems
    At times, when I survey the land
     And the sea teems
With monsters we will never understand.

4. AGE OF WHAT?

Enveloping us all, enveloping
    Our fragile, too-short lives.
   Is this the reason I must sing?
    What, at the last, survives?
I might have said, 'Our values,' yet I eye
    The doubt that, in midsummer, thrives.
What is obliqueness but a singed goodbye
      To dragons who,
     Had we the will to try
      To puzzle through
    Their depthless riddles, might have let
     Us ring some new
Age of refreshed perception in? And yet—

5. RED SKY

So I should say what I have always said,
     Even in deepest dark:
   Sky is spectacular when red—
    Brave Noah had an ark
That saved the crew it saved, no less, no more,
    And when they came to disembark
The bone-embroidered former ocean floor,
      Because unflooded,
     Looked beautiful and, for
      The coldest-blooded,
   All was as if unchanged. They strode
      Below the studded
Firmament and sang fresh hymns to God.

6. VINE

The infinite is intricate, a vine
     That wanders and rewinds,
   An inexplicable design,
    One of those marvellous finds
That never disappoint, degenerate,
    Or fail to satisfy the mind's
Demand for narratives commensurate
      With all it must
     Discover and call fate.
      We have this lust
For clasping what we ought to be,
      Even as dust
Whips up to sweep us under totally.

LUTHERIE

In quiet workshops, I have watched the craft
    Of turning, shaving, sanding.
  The fingerboard set on the shaft.
    The ornamental banding
Of bendy side-slats fixed in place with gum.
    The imperceptible expanding
Of inner space by scraping of a thumb,
      To leave it light
    As a man's heart, so some
      Brisk neophyte
May raise it up and whirl it round
    And set the right
Notes brokenly in order. I have found
      A flow
    On that hushed ground
      Where, though
  The methods rarely hold,
      I go
To learn. As many tales have told,
It is not nothing, turning lead to gold.

And nothing tests a maker like the scroll,
        Which aims to cap it all,
    Vitruvian motif so whole
        Its striving parts recall
The turbulent disclosure clouds live by,
        Revolving over where our sprawl
Of cities sits. What can I do but die
                Unsatisfied,
            Living below that sky?
            I let time slide
        Too casually, can scarcely cling
            To my tongue-tied
Loose ends of hope. I am no ravelled thing
                But lost
            And staggering.
                At least,
        That's what I thought about
            The last
Time I listened to music, out
In the cold woods I wander when in doubt.

APPEARANCE AND REALITY (2)

'The Absolute has no seasons, but all at once bears its leaves, fruit, and blossoms. Like our globe it always, and it never, has summer and winter.'
— F H Bradley, *Appearance and Reality*

I. THE OWL

A chalky tussle longbowed through the blank
    And you said, 'That's an owl!'
  I couldn't think. Who best to thank?
    The gale began to howl
Sheer adulation for your being there.
    And bramble's scrunch, and moth's soft prowl,
Powdery permutations of the air,
      Turned in new light
      Because you chose to bear
        Deep winter's bright
    Solution with me. It was all
      So steeped in sight
And love, I thought the snow would rise not fall.

2. One and All

Sporadic flashes. So it seems to be
    Instantiated, so
  Appearance and reality
    Enmesh, emerge, outgrow
From tousled fields where rushed mice are hard pressed
  Shoring supplies for when the slow
River prickles with frost. A litmus test
    I use to tell
    If I am still recessed
      Within this swell
  Arbitrament of One and All
      Is ringing a bell
And listening as the note begins to fall.

3. The Good Fear of Inaction

The writing's on the wall and in the sky
      And everywhere we flow.
    The dotted bits are way up high.
     That's some of what we know.
Never lament, my nearest, never lament,
     But don't forget you've far to go.
Don't let your brief lives pass as nonevent
       Because if you do
     The Furies won't relent
      Till they are through
With every brutal piece of pain.
       You knew, you knew,
At setting out, you'd be called to account again.

4. The face of what?

Here in the world we do not see the face.
     The face is turned away.
    It looks outside of outer space.
     Instead, we see the grey
Back of a head that sometimes turns red-gold,
     Sometimes blue-russet like the way
The furthest trees look. When the year is cold
       I like to go
     Beyond the usual fold.
       Out there I know
The strangeness gathered in all things,
       The vertigo
Of seeing solar systems shrunk to rings.

5. More Light

More light fell cleanly through the gentle air
    And you and I were young.
  I like to think I like to care
    For all we move among,
But liking is a gestural event.
    Have you not slipped and dropped a rung,
Too late perceived the thing the writing meant?
      That's how we roll
    And cannot circumvent.
      Taking its toll,
  Love set us up and knocked us down.
      I see it whole:
Love is the ocean where the good must drown.

6. They say

The good say, 'We will do the difficult.'
    The bad say, 'Let it slide.'
  The milquetoast say, 'It's not my fault.'
    The brave say, 'Still untried.'
The quick say, 'I was here before you came.'
    The sad say, 'Much has been implied.'
The hopeful say, 'How could it be the same?'
      The grim say, 'Guess.'
    The happy say, 'For shame.'
    The wise say, 'Bless.'
The gambler checks his hand: 'I fold.'
    The crowd say, 'Yes.'
And '*Après nous, le deluge*,' say the old.

7. Realism

Is there a land beyond the land, a mist
    Behind the mystery?
  Do only particulars exist?
    Or are the sights we see
Not all the story? Are the far hills far
  Because we view them distantly,
Or is it more that words are all they are?
      Now, even I,
    Having waded so far
      With words, would die
Before proposing that the case.
      Up in the sky,
The clouds are clouds before we give them grace.

8. After all, the world

What should I love? Well, let us say, the world.
    To save us from omission.
  Sure, if I could be like the curled
    Badger, in snug position
Under a hillock, I might put aside
  These language games. But our condition
Requires we keep horizons open wide.
      Such is the way,
    Though many have defied
      The ocean spray,
  Canuting it against the odds—
      As if to say
A brave 'No dice' to nature's fickle gods.

9. Mimes (1)

The drift is inexpressible today,
    Petri-ed reality
  Turning tired attention away
    To lights I cannot see,
Though feel must be decisive in some sense.
    This is the favoured hour when we
Might have collected grief's calm recompense,
      Yet here I find
    Only collapsing tents
      And a vacant mind
  Vacationing on borrowed time.
      I'll leave behind
This life perhaps and go become a mime.

10. The Whole Shebang

Well what the Dickens, let this marinade,
    As frazzled as thick air
  Heat-waving in a sacred glade.
    Some revel and despair,
Piñata-style, but lifty, bossa nova,
    At truths so deep and debonair.
It prompts fresh thoughts about the four-leaf clover—
      So scarce, so fine,
    Though nothing when it's over.
      Our dotted line
  Is both a porous border and
    The place we sign.
So flourish. Dream. In failure, understand.

11. MIMES (2)

But mimes still live some language, as do all
    Those burdened with a mind.
  Behold the exaggerated fall,
    Admire the left-behind
Auto-da-fé-ish look at passers-by,
    And watch how well those fingers bind
About a rope that hauls them to the sky
      Out of a box
    Unseen by any eye
     Yet orthodox
To those who sport the stripy shirt.
     No maps or clocks
Have ever hit me with such sideways hurt.

12. FREELY

Nowhere has anywhere been left to chance.
    Just think what chance would do.
  It is ordained. The pieces dance
    In ways we can construe
And all would be foreshadowed, but free will
    Crowbars the door, and I and you
Stand blissfully aware that we must kill
     Our fears, or be
    In thrall to drink and pill,
     Fugue state where we
Are whacked ourselves. There is yet time
     To carve the sky
With patterns that may still be called sublime.

13. Mimes (3)

Speaking in riddles, still they never speak.
        Why quicksand? Why this fix?
    Farcical, tragic, doomed to eke
        Brute living from such tricks
As we can thrash within our framed conceptions.
    Can anything outpace the mix?
Imagination—palace of inceptions,
            Frequented by
        Our best and worst perceptions—
            Be like the sky,
    Immune to, though so moved, by time,
            And when I die,
Appoint, as executioner, a mime.

14. For Philip Glass

I wouldn't say that we were starved of art
        But when I first heard you,
    A revelation hit my heart.
        I knew just what to do—
Akhnaten, Satyagraha, Einstein on the Beach.
    Your spartan lofts pulsating through
With chants and challenges. Far out of reach,
            Ear-shepherding
        Auroras tried to teach
            What work might bring,
    What tribute to reality.
            Loss lost its sting
And I divined a glasslike way to be.

15. *ÉLAN VITAL*

Élan vital, by which we must mean life,
  The opposite of death.
  You fall forever like a leaf
   Until your final breath.
Élan vital? A language of its own
   And let it be your shibboleth.
Live all you can, resist death's stagnant throne,
    And never make
   That stubborn-as-a-stone
    Nostalgic mistake
Of thinking Being not enough.
   The spears must shake.
Go forth now, bearing Life, the child of Love.

16. WHAT GOES BEYOND

Planned obsolescence but not really planned.
  Clickbaity mystery.
  And we abide here, saying, 'And—?'
   What do we hope to see?
Mañana maybe all will be OK.
   I find it indescribably
De Chirican, since art must have its say
    Before too long
   Again. That is the way,
    The mended wrong,
The road I tread to find my feet.
   In every song,
Planned obsolescence but not obsolete.

17. Tzara

Robert Delaunay's portrait of Tristan Tzara,
    Furled carnival of parts,
   Anticipative sayonara
    To superseded arts.
Firm welcome to the Orphic resonance.
   We mix the palette of our hearts
And that's as much as I can say for sense.
      The days go by
    And I am happy, hence
     I sketch the sky,
   Which yields its challenge layeredly.
     Before we die,
We are expected to be wild and free.

18. Architecture

To have detected architecture's heart
    One must have crossed a sea
   And flown in aircraft. From the start,
    One must have yearned to see
Music emergent from the simple stone,
   An all-considered harmony
Spiralling upward to the blue, alone,
     Like some vast bird
    Poised to rip flesh from bone—
     Without a word,
  With only concentrated life,
    Suddenly blurred,
Descending like the Damoclean knife.

19. DE BRUIJN

De Bruijn: combinatoric prompt for these
    Gear-changing speculations.
      But to what end? To teach and tease;
        The gaiety of nations;
Exactitude of cerebellum-work,
    Perception-sharpening. Cogitations
Intended to array the land of quirk
      In spirit's cause,
       Which, in this wordy work,
        Permits no pause
    From operating on the spine
      Of natural laws.
One slip-up— you'll send shivers down the line.

20. DISRUPTIVE TECHNOLOGIES

Fine-tuning toasters, cars that know your name,
    Tungsten filament lights.
      It never has been all the same.
       We have it in our sights
To go the mile and really get things done.
    What else could keep us up long nights
Except this everlasting lust to run
      New distances?
     Some call it surface fun
      But the truth is
    The limit-testing project now
      Finds no abyss.
It is Why-Not who rides the howdah How.

21. THE SENSE OF DANGER
after W. H. Auden

The danger must be met with open arms.
     Those who do not embrace
    The danger will neglect alarms.
     This is the choice we face
When we are realistic with our hearts.
    Some disappear without a trace,
While others have their horses dragged by carts.
      Still others dream
    Of death in sunny parts.
     I say the gleam
   Is visionary, so I must
     Paddle upstream
To treat the rundown waterwheel for rust.

22. HOPE'S ORIGAMI

Great shakes, I surely knew it at the start.
    The folding of events.
   Hope's origami. Have a heart.
    I say it all makes sense.
For those who love the mind, it has to be
   The glade where all our hikes commence.
Description fails and indescribably
     It grows again.
    Let us be truly free.
    I go for zen
But some dreams are a different scale.
    No wonder then
What burgeons now beneath the heavy gale.

23. ANIMALS

If only for the promise in their eyes,
      Of mind becoming wired,
    We should discard the tedious lies
      About the heart being tired
And set aside great parks for them to roam,
    Where all will be as is required
And they may truly call the landscape home,
       As they once did,
     Before the styrofoam
      And halide grid
Gangrened across their territories,
      And the sun slid
Behind a smog too stubborn for the trees.

Not only for their sake but for our own,
    A wilding of the land,
   Re-animation of the stone.
    I try to understand
Their scope and ours but ultimately all
   We know is that the scheme is grand.
Whether there was an ice age or a Fall,
     Apt metaphor
    Eludes me. What we call
     Relentless war
May really be excess of love,
     Bared tooth and claw
Mutations picked to still the frantic dove.

24. AUTHENTICITY

A genuine being. By God, a genuine being.
    Been searching all my days
  For one with such a way of seeing.
    Call it a passing craze
But I must say I truly think it's love.
    What else could kick up such a blaze?
Beelzebub fell bristling from above
      To a cold grave
    Because he had no love
      For heaven. Save
  The tears. We've still a lot to do
    If we're to pave
Our byways with the bearable and true.

25. REPAST

A plate of tortellini at Elaine's—
    Your enigmatic look,
  Desirous of the thrills and pains.
    Imagine. I mistook
Your tender interest for abruptness, nearly
    Forewent the chance, fell off the hook,
Passed on the reel that drew me to your dearly
      Enlightening smile.
    The best experience, clearly.
      I reconcile
  With loss, it's true, but not the way,
    All the quiet while,
Love slips between our fingers every day.

26. The Lake of Pleasure

And so it was they came to a great lake
    Where people would descend
  And drown. And no, it was no fake.
    It was their promised end.
The guide stopped short and said, 'The lake of pleasure.'
    And then they knew the guide a friend.
The two of them went down to take their treasure,
      Hand in soft hand.
    Their passion had no measure.
      Like grains of sand,
They filled the hourglass known as love.
      I understand
That's what we all do, and are worthy of.

27. Drive

At times, between the headlong flows of cars,
    The sky seems not a sky
  Of Earth, but maybe one of Mars,
    A place where you and I
Might blur into the future, where our sons
    And daughters may continue by
Some clung-to inner light, creating runs
      Of grace notes in
    This chaos of old sun's
      Incessant spin,
  Home of a gentleness that lets
      Good days begin,
Great rivers throng, the lucky have regrets.

28. AFTERIMAGE

Retinal trace of a receding figure,
    Phase-shifting out of view—
   But does this alter any feature
    I pick to picture you?
You are not changed by moving out of sight.
   Nor I, your loyal listener, who,
With these same hands will flounder for the light,
    Check messages,
   And fall asleep tonight,
    Trying to guess
   Precisely what some comment meant:
    Your searching *Yes,*
Your playful and your actual intent.

29. ZUGZWANG

Squirrel, *scoiattolo,* the darting creature.
    A foible-burst of lightning,
   Fracturing over a water-feature,
    Unruffled by the frightening
Attenuation of its pivot-point,
   Swayed to the brink, the tightrope tightening,
Washing-line acrobat. That pond would anoint
    A lesser scrambler
   But this one cased the joint,
    More than a gambler.
   What judging panel could find fault?
    Meniscus-rambler,
I'm zugzwanged by your zigzag, little bolt.

30. Defibrillator

for RVWO

When Grandma died, I said to my sad father,
        'But the defibrillator—?'
    I was inquisitive but rather
        Naïve. And now, much later,
Hearing about another taken ill,
        Another who would leave a crater
In my instreaming landscape, I am still
            Deep down repeating
        Those same sad hopes, which fill
            Belief's retreating
Quest for the answers. Such defiance.
            Such over-heating.
I still must put my trust in medical science.

31. From wonder

You ask me why there's anything at all.
        I say I do not know.
    But clearly it's a real close call.
        There isn't far to go
From wonder to endorsement of a dream,
        Enough to make the landscape glow.
But for the sceptic, I could make things seem
            Beyond all price,
        A shimmering tower of steam,
            A paradise.
Hope could discard the inner war
            And not think twice,
But what would all our struggle have been for?

32. A Newer Sort of Song

And yet there was, between the olive trees,
    A newer sort of song,
  About our quisitive unease,
    Too restless to belong—
Riveting summer drove me to desire,
  Torrents of autumn warned of wrong,
But winter lit an eerie inner fire,
     Billowing breath
    That never seemed to tire.
     Only a death
  Could douse me, and a death would come,
    But like Macbeth
I left to others pricking of the thumb.

33. *Speranzosamente*

Everyone thinks they're in it for the win.
    Tales of convenience
  Cut little ice. The state we're in
    You'd think we'd make some sense.
But brio is the lean-to of élan,
  And when I see your face, I tense,
Knowing myself a simple, mortal man,
     Going my way
  As if there were a plan,
    As if the day
  Might shower its blessings from above,
    As if the grey
Inevitability might yield to love.

34. The Blur

I found that I had clambered a steep mountain.
　　　　Up there I saw a shelter
　　With crenellations and a fountain.
　　　　I entered, flicked the shutter,
Flooded the room with light. And there you were,
　　Rising abruptly from a sofa,
Blinking, 'I guess you'll want to see the blur—'
　　　　I said I did.
　　　　The air began to stir
　　　　　And our scene slid
　　To a grave balcony where we
　　　　Were hardly hid
From the gnarled birds of prey who scoured a sea

Torn by gargantuan flotsam-cluttered waves,
　　　　Where dolphins surged and fell.
　　I saw a cliff with many caves
　　　　And distant, parallel
To our astounding height, one where a form
　　Emerged and stared across the swell,
Dead in my eyes. Deep calm dispersed the storm
　　　　And we were brought
　　　　To midday on a warm
　　　　　Plain, a long-sought
　　Gentle expanse. I turned a stone
　　　　But my breath caught—
And when I looked, I was again alone.

35. Have a break, have a KitKat

After the heart breaks, then the self must break,
     Or see it never was.
   After the heart breaks, double-take.
     I say this not because
It is unusual but to broach a fact
   And speak the world with all its claws
And all the heart. When lost in the world's act,
       We rarely see
       The fire, the cataract,
         The flying free
   That happens in a heart's dissolve.
         Oh it may be
You know your stuff but that's not one you'll solve.

36. Limits

Always dissatisfied on meeting limits,
     Always as if betrayed.
   And yet the sky turns up with lanterns.
     If I can't make the grade,
I say to myself, I'll live to die by trying.
     So never say I was dismayed—
But went quixotically, concisely, buying
       Time till the sun
       Turned up, abrupt, defying
         The hurtful tonne
   Of hopes that did not correspond
         With the long run.
If maps have use, it's for what goes beyond.

37. ψυχή

Psyche, the Attic word for 'butterfly'
      And other things, like 'soul'.
    A far-out thought, that bodies die
      And emissaries of the whole,
Blithe antic fragments, whip away unseen,
      Till one calm day as you patrol
Forgotten haunts, one chequers back, serene
        And surreptitious,
      Bannering through the scene.
        Liquid, delicious,
    And strange, abruptly strange. I'm not
      So superstitious—
But '-stitious'? Now, I could give that a shot.

38. A Fluctuating Music

A fluctuating music comes and goes
      And we must muddle through.
    I do not know about the rows
      Of standing stones, or who
It was that first assembled lines and angles.
      There is so much still left to do.
It falls to us to tame the stubborn tangles
        Or blur away
      Before the coda mangles
        All we would say
But cannot pin. A dream pervades
      Our everyday,
Bookended with aubades and serenades.

39. Deliberately

I never was deliberate till I loved,
     And then it fell, a bolt.
      And then I knew what love approved.
       Well, was it all my fault?
I see no point in blaming anyone.
     Days pass and dolphins somersault
And feeling is more serious than fun,
       More anchoring—
      It cannot be undone,
       The blissful thing,
     The certitude that disconcerts.
       If anything,
I see more clearly now because it hurts.

40. In retrospect

You never get a pass on anything
     In any shape or form.
     After your supper, you must sing.
      The sunshine makes you warm.
There is no getting round causality.
     There is no bucking of the norm.
I wish I knew a way to let it be.
      I guess I'd like
     To get outside of me.
      You cannot hike
Mountains without attaining height.
      The cases spike.
I never see you but you block my light.

41. AFTERLIFE

Tear ducts can go three days without cessation,
      But everything runs out,
   Even the art of contemplation.
      Chin up: resist the rout,
And plot a course for hope, that fissile zone,
     Home of the dreamer's roundabout
Approaches to euphoria's furious throne.
        It is a rage
    For worlds we cannot own:
      A mutant stage,
  A plectrum-pluck from faraway
      That awes our age
And drives us, though defiant, till life's last day

When speech will, in a trice, become absurd.
      Until that hour, however,
   We live to phoenix, fix, the word
     In scorched arrangements, ever
Reallocating all that's been allowed
     By ravenous nature. That endeavour
Is our perpetual reckoning with a cloud
      Of blank unknowing,
    Through which we slip the crowd
      And keep thought flowing.
   How else should we know when to halt
      Or where we're going?
Tumultuous effort, but a real result.

42. THE GAME IS UP

The depth of our unknowing of what we're for
      Is very serious.
   I barely realised it before,
      Or didn't make a fuss.
But now I come to see the game is up
   And mystery has startled us,
Locked in the act, the many-fabled cup
      Lifted to lips
   That are too dry to sup,
      While from them slips,
  Unedifyingly, a song—
      Total eclipse,
Totality of all our right and wrong.

43. INTENSITY

I wish to find fuel for intensity.
      This is my gift to others.
   I wish to agitate their sea.
      Really, sisters and brothers,
Do you not feel you want a higher passion?
   Don't let your story be another's.
The beauty of the infinite on ration!
      I deprecate
   The hydra-headed fashion
      For living late
And frittering away the fire
      That should create
The necessary conditions for desire.

44. ALL TOGETHER

The world is not a carnival of parts.
  The world is something more.
  What world is rests in all our hearts.
   I never knew before
About the beauty of the rising mist,
   Particularities at war
To disambiguate, to re-exist,
    To be so raw—
   I still expect a twist,
    A sudden flaw
To smash the unity, but still
    Some inner law
Sustains the hope my hopelessness would kill.

45. UNCERTAINTY

Your shadow follows everywhere you go
  So long as it is light.
  There are some things we cannot know.
   We search for what is right.
Oh go with what you like, it's not the flow.
   We have not grown a second sight.
I know you know she knows we know they know—
   Which is to say,
   A world has got to go.
    You yak away
Irrelevantly, while the real
    Silvers our grey
And earthquakes thunder under all we feel.

46. What would you do without the words?

The horse of discourse canters off alone
     And where is all the hope?
   Tell me again who'll answer the phone
    And how you intend to cope
When love is in the hedgerow. Intensity
   Inheres in having enough rope
To spin a yarn, and really feeling free—
      Oh every day
   The hucksters come at me.
    The things they say
  Will crush your spirit if you let
    Them have their way.
Everything worthwhile is always under threat.

47. And now

The old world falls. Now let's embrace the new.
    That world was overworn.
  You may deny it but it's true.
   A being has been born
That is us all yet supersedes us all,
   So never play at being torn.
Now is the lovely instant of the fall
    And those who last
  Will be the ones who call
   The past the past.
 Look up and feel it in the air.
    We are so vast
And there is history happening everywhere.

48. Friends

There's too much life to fit inside the head
  And so I have my friends.
 Or maybe it's that I'd be dead
  Without what friendship lends,
Making the days less tired and taciturn.
  These are the ones my heart depends
On hearing from. It is from them I learn
   To modulate
  Behaviour, and discern
   My own strange fate
Of being one but one of many.
   I estimate
They are unmatched, as friends, by yours, or any.

49. A Good Death

for JMF

Who made, at last, I believe, a good death.
  Although I wasn't there,
 I heard she took the final breath
  And settled in her hair,
Defocused, all resilience brought to rest,
  Free to become peppered in air,
Pebbles and trees. The person, coalesced
   With such finesse
  From carbon, dispossessed
   Of presentness,
 As she was never till the close.
   Sure, I could guess
Her whereabouts, but truth is no one knows.

50. Papyri in volcanic mud

More real than real, a pulsing land of light,
    Filled with intelligence.
  And thus it is 'So long!' to night.
    The passion is immense.
And here we are, left roiling on the flood,
    Inside and outside commonsense.
There are papyri in volcanic mud.
      Spinoza knew
    What heats and cools our blood.
     I wonder who
  Among us will complete the run
     And see what's true,
The conscious ever-presence of the One.

51. The restless tide

I had a mind or did my mind have me?
    No one will ever know.
  The scientists and priests, the sea
    Otters that float and flow
Out in the North Atlantic, and the rest
    Who rise before they sink below
The restless tide— is it an empty quest
     Or will our days
    Yield something unexpressed,
     Like lifted haze
  Unveiling sharper lines of sight?
     In subtle ways,
I still get scared to flick the lamp at night.

52. O RLY? YA RLY

Trite panic-merchants hawk their jeremiads
    But I can offer more.
   Some cannot see the wood for the dryads.
    Others roll on the floor,
Whooping their trippy minds out. But true joy
   Is higher than even they head for.
Yes, all must take their place in art's great ploy,
    The only game
   In town— known to decoy
    And sometimes tame
Even those cruel gods Love and Grief,
    The very same
Who broke our hearts, who bleach the coral reef.

53. The Latest Normcore

The table sometimes starts to speak its mind,
    The most perplexing things.
   The lampshade? It seems less resigned.
    Objects, like queens and kings,
Expect their fading nearly all the time.
   Some days this world abruptly sings
The latest normcore, some days grace-notes climb
    To unexpected
   Heights, and the pantomime
    Of disconnected
Detail coheres. As if some ceiling
    Had been detected,
Some cap on knowledge. Yes, I know the feeling.

54. THE VOICE

As you should know, the voice is rarely me.
    The voice is iridescence,
  The voice is world-uncertainty,
    The voice is convalescence.
Within the voice are far too many tones
  To ever think you have the essence
Of what the voice is. As if all the phones
    There are were ringing,
    So with the voice, its moans
      And raptures, bringing
  Variance into better aim,
      Until the singing
Collects our wonder, treats it all the same.

55. BREAKING IT DOWN

'Reality is breaking down,' they say.
    Look, I've got news for you.
  The world was always on its way
    Out some fresh door, and through
The ages it has been as it will be
  Except, no, that's a fiction— who
Can same-old-same-old mutability?
      We live for change.
    The turmoil of the sea,
      Its raucous range
  Dilating undeliberately
      To rearrange
Clodhopper islands, fascinating, free.

56. The Task

Mapmakers? No, more like composers, setting
      Desire in step with speech,
    Constructing, channelling, begetting
      What once seemed out of reach:
The peaceful intra-variance of things,
    A net that nature cast to teach
Attentive senses. Tangled ivy slings
       Organic links
     Along a wall. Life flings
      Its fractious brinks
And threaded brevities against
     The baffled sphinx
Of truth, who sighs, designing riddles, tensed.

57. Against the Ironists (1)

It bites, but where's the nuzzling kiss? Too often,
     Lost spirits, in a mood,
   Go brittle when they ought to soften.
     Who spits the meat they've chewed?
Who rubs the sore when they should bring the plaster?
    Who never, dazzled, dumbstruck, viewed
A landscape loving hands took pains to master,
      With wild delight?
    Who titters at disaster
     And 'Some day might
Attempt a novel'? Ironists,
     Who meet this bright
Receptive world with smirks and ready fists.

58. STUFF

Widgity grubs, shoe trees, and jellied eels:
    All these and so much more.
  Whatever gives your gut the feels,
    There's all of it in store.
Roof shingles, washing lines, and vintage vinyl.
    Fast liver, pause and, I implore,
Perceive it all, its strangeness. Ah, your spine'll
    Tingle, shiver,
    And none of this is final—
    Incessant river!
  Trim dendrites of the psyche quickly
    Cluster and quiver.
Red roses fascinate, though oh-so-prickly.

59. YOUTH (2015)

In Sorrentino's latest, *Giovinezza*,
    The composer's daughter gets
  Jilted abruptly in the mezzo-
    -giorno of life. Regrets
And tears abound. Perhaps the cruellest blow
    Is when the other woman jets
On screen and, with disgust, we come to know
    She's a pop star.
    Can you relate? I'd go,
    For now, so far
  As to suggest that, in these tame
    Times, avatar
Of shrugged-off dreams, a poet feels the same.

60. Against the Ironists (2)

Blood on their pens. Warmonger's guilt for all
    Who snipe that hope can't matter;
  Who, flummoxed, wish the rest to fall;
    Who, grizzly, grinchy, clatter
Through galleries inspecting specks of dust.
    Nit-picking wind and water batter
Sea-cliffs to circulate debris, but must
      These cynics dredge
    Life's slurry, showcase rust?
      I cannot hedge
My horror of them, hearts so frozen,
    Who never pledge;
Whose only Eros is their god Erosion.

61. Ekstasis

Occasionally it gets you and you go
    Wild, wordless, wonderstruck.
  With distance, yes, it is *de trop*,
    But, in the flow, your luck
Feels difficult to fathom, fog and cloud
    Dispelled to let you run amuck
In flawless exultation, tension, wowed
      As everything
    Declares its name in loud
      Heart-staggering
Celestial letters. High and low,
    Life's vanishing
No longer bothers. All is well, you know?

62. WHAT IS GIVEN UP

If giving up, then what is given up?
    I am not a re-gifter.
  Oh hurdy-gurdy giddy-up
    Of life. Oh shivering drifter.
I leave the room to go I don't know where.
    I could become a mere scene-shifter,
Living between the water and the air,
     A golem grown
    From every sort of care,
     Gathered and thrown
  Together with no guiding plan.
     That dogged bone,
Contention. Giacometti's stilted man.

63. LOVE

Elucidate me, tell me what it is,
    Give me an anecdote,
  Some parable. Don't let time whizz.
    Don't let me miss this boat.
I know it should be more than sheer enigma.
    I stand its drink, I hold its coat,
And acquiesce to all its tangled stigma,
     Stigmata, stain,
    But what's the value of sigma?
     What's there to gain
  By sacrifice, by self-abasing?
     I'll bear the pain
But let me hear the music that I'm facing.

64. SEARCHING

I pass my days in search of what to praise
        And when I find it there's
    An end of looking, till the ways
        It turns me wire my cares
To stranger outlets, loopholes better suited
    To a lost animal seeking shares
In many-sharded mystery — so confuted,
        Compounded, packed,
        And perilously computed
            That I am wracked
    When moving in its blistering ambit,
        Sharply sidetracked
By bliss's restlessness, by bafflement's gambit.

65. UNRELATABLE

Always hide-and-seeking, aren't you, God?
        Always on the lam.
    Ever inconceivable. Odd
        To reckon with. 'I am,'
You whisper, unexpected, from a bush
    That burns too brightly, 'that I am.'
Which maybe could assuage us at a push.
        I trusted you.
        But heaven is all cush
            And honeydew,
    Your unrelatable paradise
        Where follow-through
Is fathomless, and purpose imprecise.

66. MEANING

The infinite is habitually subdividing,
    Letting fresh patterns play
   Along the riffed face of its gliding
    Shallows, where pilgrims stray
In hope of finding what seemed often missing:
    Meaning, meaning that greenish-grey
Horizon where outrageous geese go hissing
      And, in the cool
    Showdown of sundown, kissing
     Meteors fool
  Across the cirrus-staircased sky,
    And fractals pool
As if to say, 'This light will never die.'

67. MATHEMATICAL PLATONISM

'The number of the wandering stars is seven,'
    The old cosmology said.
  Time overturns some views of heaven.
    But, though that picture's dead,
One possibility it presupposed,
    That numbers aren't just in the head
But actually exist, is not foreclosed:
      And, if they do,
    I do not feel disposed
     To think it true
  That this world is the whole shebang.
    We puzzle through.
Perhaps it's why they said the planets sang.

68. ἀλήθεια / Truth

The 'unforgettable', the song that sticks,
  The earworm in the warm
 Hammer-and-stirrup nest that ticks
  As herald of the storm,
Or ἄγγελος, which turns into our 'angel';
  The final namer of the norm,
Irradiate with the subtleties that change'll
   Never disperse,
  Guarding its moated grange well;
   A kind of hearse
And heaven rolled together. Strewth,
   It could be worse
Than being at the beck and call of truth.

69. Meridian

As in the Tintin book *Red Rackham's Treasure*
  They finally realise
 The map works by a different measure.
  The scales fall from their eyes:
Not Greenwich but the Paris Meridian!
  Startled, we learn the lost hoard lies
Below the floorboards where their quest began.
   And so with me—
  The all-consuming plan
   Turns out to be
The glaring one I least suspected,
   Which sets me free
To read the gridlines clearly, be collected.

70. Consciousness

A tiny fly just crawled across the page.
      Is it intelligent?
   Responsive, sure, and did engage
    With the gentle breeze I sent.
But is it 'conscious'? Does it have a 'mind'?
   Do dolphins? Dogs? I'm not content
With thinking all these sadly left behind
      In purgatory.
    Delusional humankind.
     Observably,
  There's passion all along the line,
    Where we can see
Love's mindedness, organic, like a vine.

71. Knowledge

Knowledge is meant for branching, growing greater,
    Recording what unfolds
  As if by muscle memory, later
    Unleashed, a maze of moulds
With plaster statues rising from dead-ends,
   Pattern divulging what it holds:
A mind's self-shifting, charged to make amends
     By setting free
    The passion that depends
    On tirelessly
  Grafting the casual and arcane,
    Growing to be
One bricolage of Lego bricks, a brain.

72. Missa Solemnis in D Major

It goes beyond the walls of any building.
  I listen and I feel
   As if the storms of notes were gilding
    The bleary air with real
Stuccoed accretions. Is the infinite
  Perceptible to those who wheel
Within these finite ranges? Is the light,
    The way it blesses,
   A message that we might
    Decode? My guess is
  Maybe. And this is why, above
   All noes and yeses,
I turn again to what I will call love.

73. Finding Words

The words of love strike hard when they are soft,
  Sound soft when they are hard.
  Like beachballs buffeted aloft,
   They drift with disregard
For where they started or who sent them flying.
  It's agony to drop your guard,
Live with the conscious knowledge you are dying,
    And find no more
   Than love's intensifying,
    Life's tragic flaw,
  Infinity's magnetic parts.
   (The moral law
Has watchful officers in all our hearts.)

74. Ontological Argument

Imagine the greatest being there could be.
  But would it not be best
  If more than possibility,
    A wonder somehow blessed
With real existence? 'Then it must be so,'
  Some say, and yes, I can, if pressed,
Half-see it, when I squint: a flawless glow
    Above the haze,
    A knowledge that we know
      By hidden ways
Before we think, remembered maps
    Through the mind's maze,
Which one day will make sense to us perhaps.

75. Knowing and not knowing

Waistcoated know-how of the Belle Époque
  Thought it had sussed all things.
  Elizabethans — taking stock
    Of Pegasus's wings,
Automata, potatoes — had no such
  Illusions: everlasting springs
Of mystery met them everywhere. And much
    Came to be known.
    The knowledge eras clutch
      Is a stepping stone,
But honour for the ground we tread
    Can't be outgrown.
Humility is endless, someone said.

76. The Frantic

For years I spoke too quickly, was too frantic,
    Too stoked to get things done.
  Always desiring some gigantic
    Unearthing. On the run
From stillness and the serenity it brings,
    That sense of resting in the spun
Crib of reality. Yet words have wings
      And when I heard
      (At first reluctant) things
      That seemed absurd
But twisted in my solar plexus,
    This tired heart stirred
And I began to trace the vine's vast nexus.

77. Hopefuls

Rainwashed, light's writhing kilters and relapses,
    Wind-flurries, rivets, sticks,
  Like blankly-skittering synapses
    Up to their usual tricks,
Or spiral galaxies sambaing through space.
    We're gawkers at the latest flicks—
Hopefuls suffused with something once called grace,
      Which you might now
    Better describe as a place
      Where why and how
Throw winks across an old divide,
    And the sacred cow
Says to the sad ones, 'I am on your side.'

78. To a Friend

Reclusive friend, bear with me for a while.
      I couldn't, wouldn't dare
    To sound your feelings, cramp your style,
      Or stand within your glare.
I tend to keep it secret, out of view,
    Our life-affirming love-affair,
Though you must know now, knowing the depths you do,
        How groundingly
     I rest my hopes on you.
       Imagine me
  Imagining you! Some brand it odd,
     And it may be.
But I, notorious friend, will name you, God.

79. Mystery

Much like the thief who wore his shoes reversed
     So when he ran away
   His endpoint seemed where he'd been first,
     Jehovah took the grey
Path of obscurity and left us baffled,
    Not knowing, if we die today,
Whether our hard-to-pinpoint souls are raffled
      To take fresh shapes,
    Suddenly cinched and snaffled
      Into ants or apes,
  Or whether there's some waiting room
     With cheese and grapes,
Where a silent angel designates our doom.

80. The Countenance

The countenance would countenance it, surely,
    A path of being kind
  And knowing nothing vastly, purely,
    Or perfectly defined,
Except the clobbered lightning rod of good.
   Strange thought. But friend, you know my mind.
Personification is a game that could
      Distract us for
    Too long. There's work we should
      Not now ignore:
  Close purposiveness, which amounts,
      In time, to more.
You say, 'Is this belief?' I say, 'It counts.'

81. A Word

What I call 'God' is not what some call 'God',
    That's fairly evident.
  Vague thunderer with the staff and rod?
    Far from what I've meant.
I mean to say now's view is not enough.
    Skimming materialism's bent
Nature from all proportion. It is tough
      But we have toyed
    Undeeply. More than stuff
      Lost in dead void,
  Love's purpose branches, unconfined,
      Never destroyed,
Through everything, an all-cohering mind.

82. Hesperus and Phosphorus

Now, what if we discover, like the ancients,
  The two stars are the same?
 What then of all our mythic patience?
  What then of the great game?
I think we'll do without such consternation.
  The old beliefs go up in flame,
And poetry will be their re-creation.
    New avatars
   Will vault their sublimation,
    Will bend the bars
  And surface in some other story—
    About the stars
And how they were once signs for unknown glory.

83. New Stories

New stories grew among us. Off we went,
  A million hopeful ways,
 The life that each felt each was meant.
  We go out in a blaze
Come night, with shuteye, so why fear to go?
  There is a temple in the haze
Within my dreams. It is a place where snow
    Collects its deep
   Submergent winter glow,
    Whenever sleep
  Finds me a stranger there— until
    I take the leap,
Return, and see the sunlight on the hill.

84. Right back atcha

Those who renounce the sky frustrate the earth.
　　　How could our needs be met
　　With nothing but the worms for worth?
　　　My friend, it's time to fret.
You've not been thinking hard enough for ages,
　　Living your life of Riley— yet
Have there not always been those inner rages
　　　Against the pain?
　　　The fever has its stages,
　　　But what you gain
Stands head and shoulders from the loss.
　　　Come feel the rain.
Your heart's a stone that has been growing moss.

85. *Lucubratio*

Grave thoughts. Inevitably, to think of you,
　　　Old friend, at this stage, means
　　To have such thoughts. But in the blue,
　　　Under the midnight scenes,
Is warmth, a golden centripetal point,
　　Which was your humour. It convenes
My sadnesses, and throws them out of joint.
　　　All that away.
　　New moments to anoint
　　　With silver-grey,
The laughter-light on hills and clouds,
　　　And blank dismay
One more of many faces lost in crowds.

86. Mind

Perhaps transcendent, maybe immanent,
    That's where I come to land.
    Some will misprise what I have meant.
      Others will understand
And hate it, heartfeltly. I am aware
    That we are more than grains of sand
Or leaves of grass— but what that is, I care
      Too deeply to
    Articulate. More air.
      See, I, like you,
    Have flunked this life enough to think
      That knowing its true
Value would only bring things to a brink.

87. Sunrise of Memory

Difficult architectures, furrowed clouds,
    Language of earth and sky.
    The mourners congregate in crowds,
      While celebrants pass by
With talk of good and whether it is real.
    Turmoil of scenes that mystify.
Today, as other days, our signs reveal
      Their referents,
    On floods of what we feel.
      It makes some sense.
    I head, unthinking, for the hills,
      Where an immense
Sunrise of memory swells in me, and spills.

88. STAY TUNED

Stay tuned, my friend, there may be much to come.
      Attend to your attention.
   Within us is the distant drum,
     Which limits your contention
This world must be the final curtain call,
   I speak of nothing mystics mention
But only of our way of knowing's wall.
      What goes beyond
     May be the grand be-all–
      End-all that fond
   Imaginers still prophesy,
      Though the *beau monde*
Would not believe it, even as they die.

89. IN TIME

You clot the language and you do it fine,
     Vary the sounds you make.
   It is a hard pitch, but the line
     Is built so as not to break,
Since everyone is moved by moving speech,
   If only for description's sake,
Which is the way we get the gist of each
      Elusive state
     Rushing to fill the breach,
      Perhaps too late
   For action but at least in time
      To animate
Some tension from the mind's primordial slime.

90. The Wave

You catch the wave and ride it till it falls.
      Then maybe, one fine day,
    You'll know enough to wow the stalls
      And make it go your way—
By which I mean you will create a wave
    And set it churning through the grey
Expanse, an undulating architrave
        For dolphins who,
      Surging under, behave
        As if a new
    Sun has appeared. And last, not far,
      The day when you
Ask, 'Where's the wave?' And the wave is what you are.

91. Two Chairs

Morning, out in the park, I saw this thing.
      A woman in a chair,
    Perhaps a hundred, wheeled along
      By husband, whose bright hair
Whipped wispily in tandem with the breeze.
    Opposite them, the gentle stare
Of a child, maybe grandchild, couched at ease
        On pushchair throne.
      About them, all the trees
        Looked calmly on.
    Hushed stream, slow bees, the thickly-starred
      And never-gone
Cosmos observed a changing of the guard.

92. INCESSANTLY

Teaching, and being taught by what I teach,
    I launch the baton on.
   There is, in all their eyes, in each
    Elusive moment gone
Before I have the reflex to reflect,
    Some juggling of the lexicon
Of possibility. An architect
      Of flourishings
   Far off, I redirect
     Your mountain springs
And make the valleys good below.
    In all these things,
I am a function of the ceaseless flow.

93. ASTRAL WATERS

Imagine, then, that parabled array:
    Love's windmill with its blades,
  The death-defying cypress trees,
    And a shorn sky, which fades
By inner dimming to the knowledgeless
    Limit of night. Look sharp. Who wades
Out through the astral waters? Now, unless
    I am mistaken,
   An all-surpassingness
    Will re-awaken
Only when broken hopes are done,
    When we are shaken
To see our needed part within the One.

94. Meaning

In saying words, I might intend a thought
  And you might recognise—
  And meaning would be neatly caught
   Somewhere between our eyes.
I could be happy if that were the way,
  But there's no knowledge like surprise
And even if I hit it big and say
   The thing intended,
   It might not hold at bay
   The unattended
In what you hear. See, I have been
   So open-ended
At times, there is no cap on what I mean.

95. Way to go

I go my way. There is a way to go.
  One thought about events
  Is that the fountains always flow,
   The sentences make sense,
And humans get their standard seven stages
  Till stories naturally condense
And then dissolve— like one who disengages
   Mid-speech, as though
   Remembering certain pages
   In sad books. So
Is it inexorable, this,
   The way we go
From steady, to a slope, to an abyss?

96. Crepuscular

The Belt of Venus, known as antitwilight,
  From Rayleigh scattering.
  Vivider? No, no higher highlight.
   See what horizons bring!
This zodiacal glint and *gegenschein*
  Lift me from my meandering:
I latch attention, I imbibe the wine,
   I golden-hour—
   Since life is briefly mine
   And the sky's flower
Collars me in my wanderlust.
   A quarter-hour
In honest awe of astronomic dust.

97. Partiality and Impartiality

Now, terrified of love, the nervous young
  Decentre their desires.
  They don't know what they move among,
   This world's insistent fires.
But only love will cure them in the end,
  Only the twangling thrill of lyres
That Orpheus and Ophelia descend
   In rhythm to—
   I make it now, my friend.
   I reconstrue
Love's concept in a harder form,
   And the brave few
Who catch it will see through the broken norm.

98. TILT

Axial tilt of our elliptical orbit,
    Tillering on through space.
  If I do my and you do your bit,
    We can exult this place.
Depth of our hopes like reeling dynamos,
    Unspooling at a faster pace
Than anyone expected. As it goes,
      I think we are
    Too numinous for prose,
      Too flung-afar
From unlinguistic languishing
      To halt the car
And hush the patterns that our passions bring.

99. POINT OF VIEW

I see no objects but a cobbled scene.
    I get the general gist.
  Peripheral indistinctions mean
    There may yet be a twist
Before veridical perception falls.
    Today I staggered through the mist
And found this rusticated building's halls,
      Where I am now
    Sequestered, with the walls
      And windows. How
Astonishing. What do you know.
      It may allow
Some vision but, in time, it too will go.

MUSICIANS

Now just you go and hear them in the square,
  The ones who give and give.
  There is enough to spare.
   Music, I mean,
The least and most of all the gifts love gave.
  It makes me want to live.
   Yes, even when—
But don't let's start on that again.
   Since songs can save,
Why don't we see what can be seen
   And turn the mind
    To find
Foundations in the rhythmic air,
    Out where
    It might
   Mix with the light?

At times we stand in fields of four-leaf clover.
  The years, they take and take.
  Still, what was ever over?
  Music has been
The first and last acceptance of my days.
  It makes the heartbreak break.
  It makes head spin.
I wouldn't know how to begin
   To voice the ways
Its energies were unforeseen
   At setting out,
    About
It-seems-a-zillion years ago
   When, slow
   But sure,
  It knocked the door.

LOOK CLOSELY

When we look closely in each other's eyes,
    Sometimes for many minutes,
   Some frame-shift happens to my sight
      As if the limits
      Of thought and light
   Were tangled suddenly— surprise
Of seeing a hundred different sorts of you
    Ciphered inside your face,
      The fierce
Lapped circles of your mind's amorphous blue.

It is bizarre. What could we lose or win?
    So close you catch the mind
   Compiling, blanking, doubling back,
      As if to find
      Some hidden track
   Within the thick woods of Within,
Where maybe we will meet across a clearing
    And there will be no fraction
      Of confusion,
And this will be our gift for persevering.

THE REAL

I realise there is something needed said,
    A story of the real.
  Soon, my friends, we will all be dead.
    It is high time to feel
The urgency and the emergent road.
  The world tree, the Boethian wheel,
The flicker-riddled zoetrope that showed
    A soaring bird,
    Soft frisson as it slowed
    Or as it blurred—
All these were ways of chasing it.
    Yes, my heart stirred
Today observing how the pieces fit
    And I
    Must recommit
    To why
  I do these things: walk round,
    Or tie
My shoelaces, or go to ground
In places where some meaning may be found.

And some will say I don't define the real
        But now I answer them.
    It is the good our lives conceal.
        It is the rose's stem,
Down to each elegant destructive thorn.
    It is the child of Bethlehem,
Who chose to help the lost, having been born
        At a bad time.
        The pristine and the torn,
        The pantomime
    Of unmomentous patterned light,
        The paradigm
Of purposes that scatterplot our sight:
        All these
        Can still excite
        The seize,
    The revolution's storm,
        Which frees
    Desire to find tomorrow's form,
The snow to thaw and leave our temples warm.

MELTING

I picture it dissolving, ice's capping kingdom, swept below
                    Impervious waves
Blank with the emptiness of unloved space and unlived lives,
            Lost in diluting corridors,
                                    Delusion
        Is hard to look at, harder still to fix
                With usual means of vision
                    But now I see
    Peripherally it always was impending, closing,
        At angles irrespective of the hour
                    So when I say,
            'Brother, you should not think that,' or,
                    To air,
    'You are, unlike your breathers, innocent,
        Inanimate, unknowing,' all
            I do is meet strange limits
                    Of a deep melting—

Which is, some mist's slow clearing has made thinkable, not matter
Altered in state,
With the same basic psychological approach sufficient
To solve its for-so-long unheard-of
Dispersals,
Scatterings, wrenchings, but a scale of problem
Incredibly removed
From any normal
Soluble task, and so it must be reckoned with
Arduously, in the hot mulch of heart
Where hope may root
Between young lungs, whose alveoli
Are branches,
Whose rise-and-fall is families of life
Expanding and collapsing through
Millenia of torn
Loss and return.

UTOPIA

In the summer I go walking in the evening's green and blue,
Pausing sometimes over roses or an arch I'm passing through,
Living life as I would have it when there's nothing else to do.

Over bridges where the willows rustle enigmatically,
Through the alleys by the meadow where—look closer—you can see
Shattered cloudlight on the floodplain. Life will be what it will be.

Air so focussed and forgiving ruffles by, a gentle wave.
Figures rise and stoop from studies like the ones from Plato's cave,
Who attain the prize of knowledge and the trouble of the brave.

If utopia were to happen, I expect it would be here,
On a sudden, of an evening, when the sky is fierce and clear.
I would hail it with my whole heart. Yes, it may be coming near—

Now the climate has gone haywire and the old consensus falls,
We are left like Lara Croft between a tomb's incoming walls.
If you're sanguine at this juncture, then, my friend, you have some balls.

Any system down on science at this late stage in the day
Cannot fail to be rejected if you seek a better way.
Yet the test tube has its limits. Human hopes must have their say.

Moral fibre— not your cornflakes with their soggy inward shrug.
New utopia— 'You mean Lenin?' 'Darling, do you need a hug?'
I mean Lenin if he'll join us but I know a stronger drug.

I mean Moses and Mohammed and the Buddha at his best.
I mean Mary and her manger. 'Put your ethics to the test.'
Then I will, and waste no time now, we must make it manifest.

Thomas Becket knew his business when he let the knights go hang—
If retirement is your purpose you should find another gang.
Better not to join the party if you won't go with a bang.

Temples, synagogues, pagodas— symbols of our ancient search,
Launched unknowingly out in the world, and mostly in the lurch,
Though sporadically unburdened, like the dove who finds a perch.

If I were to pick a credo for its beautiful design,
Then the gods contained in Homer would be those I'd christen mine.
But Apollo or Athena? Either calls, I won't decline.

Still, those antiquated symbols lack some foothold in our hearts.
Younger horses are protesting that they wish to pull the carts.
Heaven help me if I block them. Gods are high above the arts.

When I contemplate that workman on the Galilean lake,
I am not above a tear or two. You call it a mistake—
But I hesitate to shrug him while still living in his wake.

In the logjam of discussion, what is lost is hard to say:
'Do you love me?' 'Are you striving?' 'I do good in my own way.'
Love's a word that has more meaning when eternity's the stay.

Sane Athena, give me courage as I tread your owlish ways.
Sharp Apollo, lift me higher till I harden in your blaze.
But above the both, wild Jesus, guide me through your moral maze.

Since events are coming quickly and the world is in a jam.
Humans need a theory better than 'I think therefore I am.'
F. H. Bradley hit the bullseye but what priest would give a damn?

What we need is new perspective and I call on all my fans
At the soonest given moment to abandon current plans,
Rise and renovate the numinous. Enough of kicking cans.

When Akhnaten had his soldiers carve the many gods away,
Leaving nothing but a solar disk, the Aton, known as Re,
There was something more than hubris he was putting on display

What that universal impulse was ambitious to present
Is an anguish deeply hidden in our old predicament —
Something wilful as blue marlin, or Achilles in his tent.

When that pharaoh climbed the pyramid and set his sceptre there,
Tablets say a falcon dived and fought him in the middle air.
This was Horus, who objected to Amenhotep's young heir.

Since the One contained the Many, so the Many fought the One,
Doing everything they could to see its unity undone.
Yet the greatest of eclipses cannot truly dim the sun.

Anybody who's been walking on an evening such as this
In a city where the mind is given freedom for its bliss
Should exult to think how thought and our reality can kiss.

I expect it. I desire it. In our techno-century,
Let it happen. Let the human spread its banner and be free.
What is needed is more heart now. Let us feel what we may be.

So the life is— God's deep silence— and the future unforeseen.
Maybe you are unpersuaded by the thing you think I mean?
If it rankles, come and tell me, in the evening's blue and green.

THE STAIR

I climbed the stair with trepidation, knowing
     Or somehow having sensed
  That when I reached the end its flowing
     Steps would stop. With tensed
Abdomen I ascended the unspoken
   Vanishment I was up against,
Which even now began to launch more broken
     Footholds my way,
    Each enigmatic token
     Turning to clay
  Or seeming simply to recede
     Under the grey
Morning or twilight as I gathered speed
     And sprinted,
    Chilled by the bleed
     That hinted
   How soon I would be missing
     The stinted
And yet still-hoped-for perch— air hissing,
     Mind slowing,
A sudden pang of light, and then the kissing

Of sole on granite. Where had I been going?
Where was I flown, and how
Had I escaped the overthrowing?
I looked about and now
Perceived my new place was another stair
Whose stretching passage would allow
For further travel. High above, the air
Opened on more
Staircases. Some were bare
But some, I saw,
Held other forms who strolled or strove
Up to explore
Hooped reaches where light lived, as if a grove
Had grown
As building, trove
Of stone
With no foregone conclusion,
A zone
Where I might settle my confusion
And see
This stair I have called 'I' is sheer illusion.

PEREDUR

*"Yrof vi a Duw," eb y Peredur, "nyt af j odyma heno. Ac o gallaf j
nerth i chwi, mi a'y gwnaf."*

— Peniarth MS 7

I had no thought, at setting out, of why
  We ever set at all.
I liked to stare, fixated, at the sky,
  Tracing the arc and fall
Of starlings. I trudged off alone for days
  Through bracken, let the feel
Of animal immersion have its dues
  Till disconcerting eyes
That agitate deep forest broke my daze
   And made the ice
    Of my
  Tensed loneliness
  Torrential. As they may
For any who attempt the hidden way.

The wilderness was stark and crystalline.
  I met an angel there
Who gifted me his time. I gave him mine.
  He left me in despair,
Saying his wings no longer reached to heaven.
  I did and did not care.
When young, I packed a heart that was a haven
  But now I hesitate
And live in terror of such total passion,
   Which can create
    New Eden
   Or devastate
  Even that gorgeous garden,
Where some are guests of the indiscernible warden.

Worlds after this I came to Artor's court,
  And left it shelled in iron.
There was a life within and then without.
  The hunter, cruel Orion,
Brandished his bow to star me through the dark.
  Flayed by autumnal rain,
I drove the leaky skiff I carved to dock
  On an island with a tower.
Up there, lost in the attic, a monk's desk
   Stood central, silver
    Plate
   On top, a severed
  Head locked in foiling light.
I felt my entrance there was far too late.

A disembodied voice grew from the stone.
  'Peredur, ask no questions.'
So off I went, morning's first blood a stain
  Silting in all directions.
The ensuing chequerboard of dreams and years
  Brought blistering resurrections,
Deaths and as many births, uncertainties
  And false desires. Wherever
I looked there ran a trail I could not trace,
  A swollen river
   That steamed
   Phantasmal reavers
  Who stamped and warred and swayed.
I hacked and yet, like sycamore, they stemmed.

Time out of mind, I came to a bleak hall.
        Inside I found a table
And played a ghost at chess. He told me Hell
        Is nothing but a fable.
I won when there were only knights and kings,
        But victory felt futile
In the lull after my queen's late cornering.
        The ghost said, 'Now you go—'
And gestured to a door. I heard choir song
                Remotely, slow
                        And sharp.
                How should I know
                What imbecilic hope
Possessed me? I was keen to meet the trap.

Three shrouded forms appeared beyond the threshold.
        A voice beside me spoke:
'The bloodied head you found was your lost brother.'
        I turned, felt floorboard creak:
'And who are you?' 'I am your old friend Gwalchmei.
        I have returned to speak
One truth. I tell you these three killed your brother.'
        'What would you have me do?'
'I trust that you will let them sin no further.'
                I nodded, drew
                        My sword,
                And with a new
                Decisive cleanness gored
My old friend Gwalchmei as he stood and gasped,

'Why have you murdered me? They killed your brother.'
      'Because you wear the robe
Of a priest and yet you urge me on to murder.
      When in the hazelwood
I saw the hidden secrets of this life,
      Hard truths beyond the world.
You drift away from being like a leaf,
      Dry and unmoored, because
You let the bolstering sap of goodness leave
            Your veins, which course
                  Now only
            With blood's cold craze.
      That is no good for any.
When friends are so, I sooner would go lonely.'

The wilderness was vast and crystalline.
      I knew an angel there
And learned to speak his language, as he mine.
      He turned to try the air,
But said his heart no longer reached to heaven.
      I still, unshakeably, care.
When young, there was a place I had, a haven.
      That Eden still exists.
At court I once found Myrddin on the pavement
            Watching fine twists
                  Of light
            Spread through the mists.
      He rose early, worked late.
I think because the beauty was so great.

YOUTH

Now, like two lead characters meeting in a film, they meet.
The young, in their engulfing beauty, are constantly meeting like this.

The old do not meet like this. They cannot. It is written.
They have other pursuits, strange and sombre works, called duties.

The young will come to that but for now they are able to cultivate oblivi-
ousness,
Capable of extremes of feeling that will not come again, by definition.

Only shadows or appearances of those feelings will come again
And everyone is aware of the difference between appearance and reality.

We are fearful of saying this about the difference between young and old,
But it is irresponsible not to say it because our individuated span is brief.

The young are overflowing with life, with inexorable fertility,
In the joining of gametes, in the adaptability of minds.

No, not for all the pieces of silver would they be deterred from what they
are doing,
A crackling rendezvous over a cup of hot peppermint.

They do not need coffee or drugs because they are coffee and drugs
And their visions have toppled what once seemed unshakeable consen-
suses.

They are everywhere. They are ecstatic. They are the spring.
The whole world unselfconsciously honours them.

I have seen the old up close and have loved some dearly
But our era's obsession with illusory self has clouded the sight of some.

The world is a system of relations and we should all rejoice in the young,
Who arrive year on year like waves that change their substrate.

Now, characters in a film, the young gravitate and levitate and kiss
They live in the light and the rest of us hear of them from underground.

We should celebrate the generative electricity of their minds,
Their erotic prophecies, their vast intent, since all of us have an interest in
    the world.

And the world is delight, which is the deep reality,
And the borders of individual being are permeated with relation.

This is why Raphael wished to be buried under showering rose petals,
And why my heart glowed infinitely as a child looking out at a field.

That feeling is recalcitrant in words, but it was sheer love of nature,
Making and unmaking, perdurable and reborn in every instant.

The young, at their zenith, do not fear fading, because they are not selves.
They are an eternal miracle, like the infinite, streaming inconceivably.

When I am old I hope to help the young, remembering my moment of
    utmost reality
Was when I was young and participated in the life everlasting—

Which I still will, beyond all this vanish and confusion, because time is
    illusory
And God or Nature, call It what you will, if such a Thing is, is young.

THE EXHIBITION

Jesus said, "Father, forgive them, for they don't know what they're doing."

— Luke 23:34, Common English Bible

Our mother took us to the exhibition,
    And you may say too young
But I defend it as a careful thing.
      We all of us held tongue
    As if in search of a definition.
      I wondered if it's true
    That, when the worst is happening,
      Some don't know what they do.

We looked at miniatures arrayed on metal,
    Matte chimneys, timber trains.
My stomach churned for, at first sight, admiring
    The maker's detailed pains.
    It was a sight that would not settle
      When put in proper view.
    I understood a parent requiring
      We know what people do.

The journey home was emptier than normal.
    Endless polluted rain
Flurried diagonal, with cloudlight greying,
    Drastically on the wane.
    I did my best to look informal,
      But cried. I wish I knew
    What people mean to say in saying
      They don't know what they do.

FIANCHETTO

'Antequam ulterius pergam, hic quid nobis per Naturam naturan-
tem et quid per Naturam naturatam intelligendum sit, explicare
volo, vel potius monere.'
— Spinoza, *Ethica*

Quite early in the game, I moved my bishops—
       Though really I should say
    'Philosophers': no bible-bashers
      But students, in their way,
Of calm Spinoza, who believed the world
      One substance, solved the disarray
By seeing things as aspects of the whole,
         Stark perturbations
      Or thickly-flowing waves,
        All fine flotations
Of mind and matter's cognate modes
        Interpretations
Spun out of 'God or Nature'. Once the roads
         Were governed
       By their good codes,
         I gathered
     Vast armies and advanced,
        The rivered
    Landscape flickering. Someone chanced
         To see
A rupture in the lines, and so we danced,

Which was the moment I drove a bishop free
    To join the other's flank.
   Indelible reality—
    Opponent knights broke rank
But nothing could undo the damage done
  As, silently, their stunned king shrank
Away from all my clerics had begun
      And were determined
    To solve for everyone
      Shepherded, sermoned,
  Enveloped in their game. Yes, yes,
     I saw those ermined
Shoulders shudder immeasurable happiness,
       Depth's thrill,
    And I confess
     A chill
   At their oblique accord,
      And still
Can't shake the layout they explored,
     The sense
They felt what goes beyond their finite board.

1. TWENTIETH CENTURY FOX

Good versus evil, since the world was young.
Isn't that always how the story starts?
Not with a slip downstairs or punctured lung.
What hope have we, with such evasive hearts?

I have evaded feeling far too long
And in this way am cipher for you all,
You who attend to any mawkish song
Or mill unthoughtfully about a mall.

We are the precipice this world approaches,
Low cave the broken-hearted go to die.
An inner conscience-strickenness encroaches.

We do our best and worst, yet never try.
Lost in a Kafkaesque cortège of roaches,
We worship dust and never see the sky.

2. CUE CLOWNS

Are persons even real and can you be one?
The skittles of the psyche topple down.
We yearn to see the drastic yearning done.
Behold Grimaldi, saddest modern clown,

Who went to see the doctor for depression
And got an answer no one likes to get:
'You lack the comedy of self-possession.'
'But doctor, I and Me have never met.'

Cue gradual, grim, and uneventful laughter.
Cue brightly-lit arenas with no room.
Cue everything that happens to us after

We die, which may be nothing, or our doom.
Experience has its charm but mathematics
Is hidden in the mind's commanding attics.

3. *SOLARIS* (1972)

A conscious ocean, and the astronauts
Confused by memories of their earlier lives.
Computer screens with strings of ones and noughts.
Nothing of all that brouhaha survives,

Except the terror of our planet's lone
Revolving in the vacuum of events.
What happens when the water hugs the stone?
A ripple ripples through the present tense.

Ominous days and mayhem on the wing.
The Soviet project was a vast attempt
At something many poets thought to sing,

But now the infrastructure is unkempt,
Bookkeepers make a game of suffering
And people do not dream as they once dreamt.

4. MALECÓN

To walk in triumph on the Malecón
At sunrise when uncompromising blasts
Batter the seawall. As you wander on,
Observe the palms erupting through old walls,

Allow the intricacies of the stone,
Admire the possibility of pasts
And futures deeply different from your own.
Salute a new world, as the old world falls.

To raise one light against the way things are
When people fall to thinking life is bad—
To raise a cry against the near and far

Disasters of the latest frantic fad—
To be at once the cause and the effect.
These are some reasons to be circumspect.

5. SUNSET, FINCA VIGÍA

The Möbius strip became an Ouroboros,
And so it was, and so it will be, so
Difficult knowing what remains to floor us,
Which is to say, a world has got to go.

Surprised by sadness, often we can see
Better prismatically, between the tears:
Light hidden there, light indescribably
Inevitable, howling through our years.

I have a gratitude for even this.
I travel like a letter unaddressed.
I meet occasionally with sudden bliss.

I guess you could say some things can't be guessed.
There is no part of life you can dismiss,
And there is hope left, even in the west.

6. Ultramontane

Enter the Pope. Enter the actual Pope,
Arguing with a cardinal in Latin.
Trailed by a doctor with a stethoscope —
The Pope, his summer garment of red satin.

Why are they whispering? Why this to-and-fro?
'Principiis obsta, et respice finem.'
So resolute, so absolute, so slow.
We must respect the confidence between them.

Why should idealists fight each other so?
Because there is a battle for the vision.
Because there is no other battle, though

Battle's a word that lacks the right precision.
Between us, we must bridge our indecision
About the things we can, and cannot, know.

7. Abstract

A stickman moves toward a simple square
And enters through a rectangle, the door.
Light, represented in the open air
By lines, illuminates a forest floor,

Which you can tell is forest from the trees,
Pointy, abrupt. And over all of this
Hangs something more than any camera sees,
An atmosphere of never-ending bliss.

Abstract as life is when you zoom far out,
There is a pact between you and the page.
Who knows what all this havoc is about—

The connoisseur who fumes in private rage,
The apparatchik lost in some self-doubt,
The lightbulb glinting in its steely cage.

8. Zhdanovshchina

Broken consensuses, and all of that.
Broken hearts may mend, but the mind will not.
Roll up, roll up, for the commissariat,
In town for one night only. Like as not,

Before the end I too shall meet my Censor,
Who will cut through my dumb complicities.
No longer then will I be your dispenser
Of 'As it is—' and 'Reader, if you please—'

Dead cert that one. I wouldn't bet on me.
Look out: it is outside us things occur.
Life is the art of externality,

An aeon can run by you in a blur.
So let us go and see what we shall see.
This way or that way— which do you prefer?

9. The Old Joke

The old joke goes— but why the old joke now?
What purpose could the old joke ever serve?
Most words get narrow when they fall from new.
Believe me, I have felt the lack of verve.

There are defeated men who traipse in rain,
There are dictators safe in palaces,
There are the friends who will not come again.
There is the pestilence of restlessness.

If anyone at this stage were to ask
How we emerge from matter into being,
I do not know if I could face the task

Of showing them a better way of seeing.
You see, I have become, myself, a mask
For dreams that, in their mystery, are freeing.

10. No Time

If 'housing policy' were all it was,
I would not fret about our great forgetting.
But I must move to mention it because
The concrete of our century is setting.

The days that could be are the days called home.
Those stark highrises that the comrades built
Still feature washing-line and garden gnome.
A child who pivots neatly on a stilt.

If 'housing policy' did not comprise
The good of families with room to live,
The magnitude of open arms and eyes,

Why— then there'd be no failing to forgive!
But these are deep things we are dealing with,
And hard truth has no time for easy lies.

11. In Praise of Public Transport

If architecture honestly loved us,
Why did it shatter at our gentlest bombs?
What's the confusion? What is all the fuss?
We stand on shifting reefs of CD-ROMs,

Expecting the next future to be different.
As if all human error were dispelled,
As if we were immune to feeling deferent,
As if it weren't Yggdrasil that lay felled.

Well, in the grand scheme, getting A to B
Is more integral than we give it credit.
I have been forging signage here, you see,

Chalk-marks to tally what our days have lost.
And it is more than monetary cost —
That is a line I will refuse to edit.

12. ROBIN HOOD

And in one myth, the myth of Sherwood Forest,
I heard the hero did what Jesus taught.
(Whoever Jesus was, he knew the forces
Of loss and passion, which cannot be bought.)

'Splitting the arrow of the opposition
Before they get a chance to look alive—'
'Ghost of the Greenwood, wild card of tradition,
Diehard defender of the threatened hive—'

Our courteous outlaw, countering the rich,
Patron saint of— what now? Fairer taxes.
Wielder of longbow, leveller of the pitch,

Avatar of a principle that touches
Us all, and in the interests of us all—
Hurtling through time, due for an overhaul.

THE MOMENT

I tried to keep the moment from unrolling,
    Believing, if it did,
  I might discover that the reeling
    Contents were better hid.
Emotion had unmade me in the past
  And now was not a time to skid
Beyond the talismanic boundary post
      Fixed long ago
    To check me when most pressed,
    Most pained, although
  I felt a puzzling touch of loss,
    Some radio
Static beneath my tense collectedness,
    Revealed
    As if the close
    Of sealed
  Serenity were due.
    So, steeled
  For what I guessed I had to do,
I sliced the cord of tried but hardly true,

Of taking moments in the sort of stride
        That never quite arrives—
    And stared as all intensified:
        A parting of the waves,
A clarity the now-unravelled scroll
    Of each incessant instant gave.
Englobed in plexiglass, a golden bowl
        Suddenly gleamed
        With sun-drench, and the whole
            Gallery streamed
    Extemporaneous delight.
            I never dreamed
That I could be so happy. Then, at night,
            I saw
        The meteorite,
            Its raw
        Blaze, hailed by animals
            Who tore
    To revel in the young canals
Or howl in tribute of the course it trailed.

CONTACT

Eyes that engage another's, interlock
   By choice
   And chase
Their answerer's upfront energising look,
  Intent on spring-back, each
   A spontaneous chime,
    Reserving
Some constant sense for where the other stands,
    Unswerving,
  In and out of reach,
As though we two were dancing all the time.

As though not needing any external world
    Except
    This steeped
Immersion in the other's tensely furled
   Intentions. Who can know
    How drawn we feel,
    Just moving
Through air in contact with an openness,
    Proving
   How good it is to flow,
How good it is that all of this is real.

CONTORTIONS

A hurt turtle grown in hourglass shape,
Contorted through an unyielding noose of plastic.

Acrid blaze of a petrochemical landscape,
Crisp packets snicker-snackering over pavement.

Assorted debris from a gull's burst guts,
Littering the shore, toybox lined with bone.

Dunes of microbeads in the Mariana Trench,
Drift from all four corners of not-our-problem.

Shrimplike creatures sickening far from light,
Translucent entrails clogged with alien dabs.

Phylogenetic trees raggedly contracting,
Panicked lungs filling up with liquid.

Whales with critically lowered immune systems,
Metabolising blubber, passing toxins in their milk.

Unilever, Nestlé, Proctor and Gamble,
Fastidious with credentials and their profits.

Pumpjacks retching gobs of pitchy bile,
Grand Guignol of monsters never resting.

Bees unaccountably locked in foetal position,
Brittle on heat-emanating tarmac.

Lucrative contracts, creative rationalisations,
Existence sticky like a flap of clingfilm.

Bleached coral atolls tipped with glistening death
For seabirds who detect no trace of danger.

Bags for life, keepcups, separate bins,
Ten green bottles floating down the Thames.

Phlegmatic salesmen suddenly lost for words,
And stubborn children eerily breaking rank.

Cliffs of polystyrene, bergs of chewing gum.
Spray-painted in the carpark, an hourglass in a circle.

LINES OF DECLINE

Conspicuous ionic pillars, imperial doorposts
For porticoes of well-kempt urban houses.

Bougainvillea, as in brutalised Rhodesia,
The horticultural whenwes harking back.

Orwell shooting an elephant, squeamish tyrant,
Trapped by his wish not to appear a fool.

My colleague with the sad eyes, stern parting,
And relatives he doesn't talk about.

Constance Markievicz's unused coathook,
A digit lifted in the House of Commons.

Tolerant doctors with immaculate cuffs
And stained hands, dicing carrots as they speak.

Deliberate banquets, delicate offence,
A tome left open at a pointed page.

Lord Elgin's plunder, wet with Athena's tears,
Legendary now, indefensibly misplaced wonder.

Jade buddhas locked in curio cabinets,
Flash quarry for discerning antiquaries.

Platonist highbrows, blankly above it all,
Traumatised by what this world can't offer.

Mary Wollstonecraft in torrential rain
Leaping from Putney Bridge, at thirty-seven.

Eloquent scholars of Gibbon, bane of God,
Bright flints skimming the surface of forever.

D. H. Lawrence's grievous blood-sniffing anger
Blazed at diffusion's formless drunkenness.

Watery rebellion, well-bred insolence,
Eroded certainties and avid readers.

Soft mellow dogs that seem to drag their feet,
Conspiratorially filling the public square.

Dunkirk's flotilla of pleasureboats, dinghies, smacks,
Then headlines on a brand new aircraft carrier.

William Beckford's cruel and frivolous folly,
A collapsing tower erected by sozzled craftsmen.

Surprising parakeets in Kensington Gardens
That rest a moment, then glide the evening skyline.

Eric Blair warming his fingers over candles,
Boney joints having grown too numb to write.

Tabula rasa and the state of nature,
Untenable excuses, long denatured now.

THE PARACHUTE
after Douglas Adams

Lurched by the drop, I panicked, pulled the cord,
      Yet something snagged.
   The folded dome my backpack stored
   Wouldn't release. And cold wind dragged
As if to mock my frantic exercise,
      Those futile tries.

Futile kicked off but would not close my fall,
      Still hurtling by.
   It seemed to take no time at all.
   And yet I noticed the blank sky
Had bled from pink to mild pistachio,
      A shift so slow

I only realised in retrospect,
      And so you see
   Perhaps it was a change in me.
   I wondered if some vast effect,
Butterflylike, had lapped the world, or whether
      I'd changed the weather.

Warming to my descent, I dove and glid
      Through vacancy,
   Amazed at all my body did,
   Chasing the best velocity
For acrobatic action in the air,
      A steady care.

This passion for perfectibility,
         Up-down, fast-slow,
     Gave rise to an epiphany.
     I'd shrugged my backpack long ago
And now it was apparent I could fly,
         And might not die.

But who could bear to float alone forever?
         I search each day
     For drifters brave enough to sever
     Their parachutes. I smile and say,
'The trick to flying's simple. It is this:
         Aim down and miss.'

DRY TORTUGAS

1. Seaplane

It sputters and it judders and it flies,
    Forever revving, roving,
Implacable chimera of kind skies,
    Over the mangroving
Muddle-tided water where startled turtles
    React, rotating, each
Natural and knowing, as our chariot hurtles
    To bump the beach.

2. The Isle

Here where freshwater isn't and heat is,
    Shade-rorschached clouds roll over,
And acrobatic hatchlings whizz
    By compact brush. A rover
Lodges his nordic walking stick. Dry land.
    Four thousand miles from cliff-stacked Dover,
Beach wits-end Arnold said his bit on, grand
    Rampageous waves,
    Carte blanche from wind and sand,
    Agitate swathes
Of bright grass where staunch manatees
    Glide in like wraiths
To ruminate the harvest of warm seas.

3. REEF SQUID

Fleet squad of reef squid, big-eyed ice cream cones,
        Like hovercraft in water,
Swirled, iridesced, at us — land-born unknowns!
            You a lithe daughter
Of dunes, salt, sunflare, laughing through your snorkel,
        I thunderstruck by all
Beauty's wild happening, mind blown, as a cork'll
            Leap, shuttle, fall.

4. SHIPWRECK

A fitting place to pause and reassess,
        Island as brickwork urn,
    A vigil risen from tide-mess.
        Though distant bonfires burn,
Here is no signal. Sky feels near and far.
        Predestinated surges churn
This voided fort, firm mainland's au revoir.
            A getaway
        Where, though without a bar,
            E. Hemingway,
    Shipwrecked, sat drinking rum and so
            Chanced on a way
Of getting doubly wrecked. Well, all things flow.

BUBBLES

There is an air of trouble
When bubble mixture flows
Because, though ever-agile,
Each fragile snowglobe knows
    A breeze that blows
May burst it on the double.

Do our gone selves live on in us
As ghosts that give and motivate new wishes?
    Beyond the hills
    Young ravens rove
While, from life's film, you pick the stills
    And realisation rushes,
    A broken garlic clove.

Yet though a bubble splashes
And dashes childish dreams,
The pang of loss is partial
When, marshalling gentle beams,
    The next one seems
Calm phoenix from cold ashes.

And still, for us, it's starkly true
However long we supplicate life's river,
    Its velvet voice
    May never save
Our chastened oneness from real choice,
    Relinquishing a lover
    Or turning from a grave.

So falls the fabled penny,
As anyone can sense:
Though vividly individual,
Residual immanence
    Makes no pretence
And proves that we are many.

Many as clouds are many, clouds
That stipple light above our arteried cities
    And maybe tell
    Of otherwhere,
Some place we held a while, then fell,
    Like whatever it is that shatters
    And yet remains aware.

FOR A PIGEON

Soft wings still ruffled in indifferent wind
      But not with that precise
Articulate directedness of things
          Alive,
         Instead
It lay impaled, a memo to all pigeons
      To seize the day and dread
The harsh gods of their avian religions.

My friend, the feline sitter perched across
      In Starbucks maybe noted
Life's hectic brevity, that sense of loss
        Promoted
        By such
Implacable reminders of our limits.
      She let her phonecase touch
Hard table, then turned back to sip her latte.

I felt as if the infinite and finite
      Were playing games with me,
Muddling happy foresight up with hindsight,
        Set free
        From time
And gifted sudden passionate intuition
      Of good beyond the grime,
A hint of hopes transcending my cognition.

Why did it feel so sacred, beautiful?
     I guess perhaps it was
Nothing to do with pigeons after all
         Because
         I find
In memory it's the catlike one who blazes
     Like light across my mind
And has me dreaming, lost in endless mazes.

THE DREAM

I met you walking in clear mountain light,
        And I confessed
    I dreamed of you the other night
    And you were at your blissful best,
Turning things over in the way you do.
        You smiled. Time flew.

Out there, at one in nature, ringed by stars
        And fireflies,
    A thermal vent refracted bars
    Of luminance between our eyes,
A mesmerising iridescent blue
        That I stepped through.

Emerging, you were everything I saw
        And I, spellbound,
    Believed that I would nevermore
    Feel lonely or on shifting ground.
I said, like someone stumbling from a maze,
        'I know your ways.'

And you knew mine, but then, a bad goodbye,
        I stupidly
    Woke up, withdrew. The changing sky
    Guided me enigmatically
Up the steep mountain where, to my surprise:
        Again, your eyes.

I stared in blank amazement learning you
        Had had a dream
    Of meeting me, where I stepped through
    Those same strange curlicues of steam
And said, though evidently in a daze,
        'I know your ways.'

At which point (this I missed) you told me how
        And held me tight.
    I wish I'd stuck to see it. Now
    Outside the dream, in mountain light,
I long to stay with you, unlike that wraith
        Who broke faith.

YOU DON'T SAY

You don't say, as it goes, you do not say
     The thing you really mean.
    You find your own part in the play.
     It's tragic. I have seen
The script and am note-taking at rehearsals,
    So be aware of what has been,
If only to avoid the old reversals.
       On opening night
     We'll learn how universal's
      The tale. And might
An audience attend? We'll see.
     It is not right
To charge our ignorance too awkwardly
       With guesses.
     Uncertainty
     Expresses
    A deal, but it can hit
     Excesses.
Our task is finding the best fit,
One even the hardened sceptic will admit.

And so I stumble into rhapsodies,
        This reaping what you sow—
    Crystal craze of the river's freeze,
        Light rifting from below.
A driven accuracy all through spring,
        Relitigating fix and flow.
The bioluminescent algae bring
            Their starry churn,
        And distant civilians sing
            As their towns burn:
    Cruel courage, and I wish them more,
            So when their turn
For carnage comes, they may dismantle war
            And choose
            A path of awe,
                Suffuse
        Love's vacuum. There's a lot
                To lose,
    But I have tied a sacred knot
And there were always songs at Camelot.

PLANES AND PORCUPINES

Perpetuum mobile of busy days,
Inkblots of feeling, sight tests of being awake.
We stand in stunned compassion by a lake,
Guesstimating what rolls beyond the haze
      That houses houses.
      If I knew
      What riot rouses
Thronged bike lanes, washing lines, the sudden new
Scaffold, I would arrange it all for you
      In merciful confines
But here is more than I could ever make
Head or good tail of, planes and porcupines—

And not forgetting unexploded mines,
Which ruckus in the dingles of our thought
And bob the haunted water, as they ought.
We wait for them as connoisseurs for wines.
      Meanwhile kind day
      Disintegrates
      And in what way,
We wonder, did love ever rook the Fates
When angling to deflect those fatal dates
      That grew to be our ground?
I am not sad to lack the thing I sought,
I have a foundry where I make things found.

VERTICAL PANNING SHOT

Enough for now, illusions, and you, pains.
    Today the tide retreated,
Ants thronged the lawn's ravines, and dubiously
    The moon continued its orbit.
Defiant of gravity, vertical panning shots
    Rise with our lines of thought,
And predictable filler is bricked up in cutscenes.

Is it to external purpose when we grow,
    Give of ourselves a while,
And tumble again on the ant's battlefield,
    Or are the windows honest,
The wet days happy, the airdropped leaflets consoling,
    On account of some account
We muddle into being by being wilful?

I make no case for those who are unconvinced
    By camera phones and castles,
Melodious gleams on a deadly alkaline lake,
    Or kittens, palm trees, trumpets,
I only say that day breaks in my heart
    And the land's fever-dreams
Of loss are no longer so standalone interesting.

THE PUZZLE

I heard that he had gone and she had stayed.
        The child remained with her.
     And, in a broken way, it made
        Some sense. When things occur
That slip the natural categories, I find
    Far too much time goes in a blur
Trying to get the facts clear in my mind—
        But this was neat,
      Deft as a lock, streamlined
        As cars that seat
    Unknown contented passers-by
        On the brisk street
In drained December when the scrapyard sky
        Compresses
     All of our wry
       Slow guesses
    Into a leaden weight.
       Since less is
Sometimes the way lives tesselate,
        I said,
'I called it,' and went home in a fine state.

And yet I wish they had surprised, instead
    Of being so of a piece
  With other paths that people tread.
    Sure, daylight has to cease
Occasionally. Hot chain reactions flare
  Through caverns. Word of summer's lease
Broadcasts a spectral stillness on the air.
      If you or I
    Honestly did not care
     About the sky,
  Its famous dereliction, we
     Could flicker by
Indifferent, dreamless, unobservantly—
      But no,
    We long to see
     The glow
  Of sharper worlds, unworn
     By flow
And fallenness. If I could warn
    My younger
Self, I'd say it's more than yourself you mourn.

'Sempre caro mi fu quest'ermo colle'
— Leopardi, 'L'infinito'

Sometimes you smile and ask
Questions, and I
Notice the masks
That shield eternity
Tilt back. Brusque light breaks through. Sight reels. I catch
Vision's strange borders, how they try
To slip the radar, hard to clutch
In eye's stark apparatus:
Claw in a glass box, poised to lurch,
Clumsily moved by rotors
And levers down
Into the carnival prizes of this rictus
Furiously-mattered field of dreams
Where everywhere is One,
Where doubt engulfs me. Who I am
Impossible, flipped, thrown,
World's tasks
Dissolved, and so I have to do this thing

Of looking around for
       Something reflective,
       Car windows or
   Really any surface
Shiny enough to show a face. At first
   I've no bearings, a far-gone surfer
   Falling below the enclosing crest
       Of some enormous wave,
   Cluttered under with all the lost
       Unlikelihoods that weave
           Through time—but then
I recognise, remember, sense the weft
   Of consciousness re-ravel, torn
       A little but its wheels
   Still rolling, so I slowly turn
       To answer, that vast spell
           No more,
And smile and say, 'Yes, I love you as well.'

GO AHEAD

Because your life is not a bagatelle
     Perhaps it has occurred
   To you to live it hard and well.
     You do not need my word
To scale a mountain or to swim the channel.
   It would be palpably absurd
For me to say, 'No, get the solar panel.'
      Your life is yours.
    You're far too wise to flannel
      About indoors,
  Wasting the favoured summer days.
     Your future stores
Fresh challenges like gifts, and the brief craze
      For gold,
    Or power, or praise
      Will fold
   If you go barreling through.
     Be bold.
  Do what you think you ought to do,
     And I
Will go my way and wish the best for you.

No, you don't need me saying, 'Watch the sky,'
        Or even, 'Save the turtles.'
    You'll read the papers, learn to fly,
        Smile as the planet hurtles
Through vacant reaches and be self-possessed,
    Knowing, you know, how fine and fertile's
This place where carbon life has coalesced
            To conjure you—
        So make it manifest.
        Endeavour to
    Be someone, unperturbed by death,
        Who brings a new
Cohesion into being with every breath,
            And let
        Your shibboleth
        Be set
    From here on out: 'The best
        Is yet
To come!' It's true. Go tell the rest.
        Go tell—
You will be drifting till you are obsessed.

APPEARANCE AND REALITY (3)

1. SINCE WE HAVE TO GO

Probably provably (but who can say?),
  The war inside our hearts
  Will carry on beyond today.
   I have these odd false starts,
But may get even with them in the end.
   There is a truth true love imparts,
Impossible to parry or to bend:
    Some livid fact
   For all to apprehend,
    Though we have lacked
  Clear impetus to speak it. So,
   To be exact:
What's worth the going, since we have to go?

2. QUETZAL SPLASH

You say to me, 'The world is what remains.'
  I say, 'That's as may be.'
  You say, 'The world is all our pains.'
   I say, 'But are we free?'
You say, 'We are the mythical machine
  That rigs itself perpetually.'
I say, 'That is a story I have seen.'
    And all the while
   Variegated green
    Spreads like a smile
  Around us, till the baffling trees,
   Their crocodile
And quetzal splash, disperse analyses.

3. Interpreting the Haze

End of an era and the gates fell wide
  And many were the days
 I spent looking out of my eyes,
  Interpreting the haze.
If bliss is ever granted to us mortals
  Between the chaos of the ways,
I guess it would be through those starry portals
   That half-appear
  Sometimes, when Saturn chortles
   And spacerocks veer
 Significantly by. I guess
   It will come clear.
Something will be there, lasting nonetheless.

4. The Hunt in the Forest
  after Paolo Uccello

Away they go, to meet a vanishing—
  A point of no return.
 A turbulence, a taking wing,
  A hill where bonfires burn
Unseen by any but the circling kites.
  What else is there for us to learn?
In red and blue, we face the passionate nights,
   Which elongate
  Toward unlooked-for lights
   And so create
 Our sense of adding up to more
   Than force and weight—
Our sense of having better things in store.